Streetcars at the Pass, Vol. 1

Review

The gunfighter has his flair, the gambler his cards, the shady lady her charms, the preacher his pulpit, the businessman his money box, but El Pasoans in those early days seldom left home without catching a mule-drawn streetcar. It wasn't the trusty horse or the pointy-toed boots that moved the average El Pasoan from one part of town to another; it was the mule-drawn streetcar. And this is the story, told in part from the mule's point of view.

Ron Dawson is the premiere authority on early day El Paso's streetcars, whether mule or electric-powered. Of even more importance, Ron Dawson has devoted a lifetime of love and research to the subject of this city's initial form of transportation, perhaps the first mule-drawn international streetcar line in the world.

…Leon C. Metz, author of *John Wesley Hardin, Dark Angel of Texas*, Western writer, historian, and lecturer on the History Channel.

Streetcars at the Pass, Vol. 1

◆

The Story of the Mule Cars of El Paso, The Suburban Railway to Tobin Place, and The Interurban to Ysleta

Journal of the Railroad & Transportation Museum of El Paso
No. 1

Ronald E. Dawson

iUniverse, Inc.
New York Lincoln Shanghai

Streetcars at the Pass, Vol. 1
The Story of the Mule Cars of El Paso, The Suburban Railway to Tobin Place, and The Interurban to Ysleta

All Rights Reserved © 2003 by Ronald E. Dawson

No part of this book may be reproduced or transmitted in any form or by any means, graphic, electronic, or mechanical, including photocopying, recording, taping, or by any information storage retrieval system, without the written permission of the publisher.

iUniverse, Inc.

For information address:
iUniverse, Inc.
2021 Pine Lake Road, Suite 100
Lincoln, NE 68512
www.iuniverse.com

No part of this book may be used or reproduced in any manner whatsoever without the written permission of the author.

ISBN: 0-595-29623-8

Printed in the United States of America

Contents

Introduction 1

Part I   *The Mule Cars of El Paso (El Paso & Juarez Traction Company)*

The Need for a Public Transit System in the 1880s 5
The Line to Paso del Norte (Cd. Juarez) 12
The San Antonio Street Line 14
The Belt Line on the American Side 19
Enter Zach White 22
Anson Mills and the Consolidation of the Mule Car Companies 24
The Clamor for Electric Cars by 1900 29
Recollections of a former St. Louis Newspaper Man 33
Mandy the Mule's Parade 36
The Last Mule Car (poem) 41
Memories of Riding the Mule Car 43
The Electric Car Era Approaches 44
The Survival of No. 1 46

Part II   *To Tobin Place, (El Paso Suburban Railway)*

Land Developers and Their New Towns 55

The Development of Tobin Place 57
The El Paso Suburban Railway 59

Part III   *The Interurban to Ysleta, (Rio Grande Valley Traction Company)*

Developing an Interurban to Ysleta 65
Construction Begins 68
Power and Equipment 70
The Decline of the Interurban 73
Conclusion 77

About the Author 79
Friends of the Railroad and Transportation Museum of El Paso 81
Acknowledgements 83
Photograph Credits 85

Introduction

Streetcars at the Pass will eventually encompass the complete history of urban and suburban rail transit in El Paso County. The first three parts are included here and cover the mule car era from 1882 to 1902; the El Paso Suburban Railway to Tobin Place, ca. 1907–1914; and the Ysleta interurban, known as the Rio Grande Valley Traction Company, ca. 1913–1925. Future contributions to this series will survey the early electric years from 1902 to the maximum size of the system in 1925, then the gradual conversion of carlines to bus routes in the thirties and forties. Lastly, there will be a history of the PCC car era from 1950 to 1974, the end of service.

In this first volume, the research into the development and operation of the various mule car companies was particularly daunting, as there were often conflicting accounts in newspapers and in historical documents. To add to the confusion, writers in the past have often only touched briefly on the history and operation of the mule cars, and then unknowingly passed on erroneous information which can be traced back to a few sources in the first part of the 20th Century. I will attempt to clarify some of those unintentional, although factual, errors. The role that the mule-powered and the electric-powered streetcar have played in the growth and development of El Paso's neighborhoods, and in providing cross-border mass transit, has never adequately been recognized.

PART I
The Mule Cars of El Paso

The Need for a Public Transit System in the 1880s

By the time of the conclusion of the War Between the States, cities around the nation were using streetcars, i.e., horse cars or mule cars on rails, for public transportation. A major early builder was the John Stephenson Company of New York. Author John White,[1] in his book, *Horsecars, Cable Cars and Omnibuses*, indicated that Stephenson had made many improvements in streetcar designs:

> "The boxy arch-roofed cars soon gave way to lighter models with pleasing swelled sides and ogee roofs. The lower panels were concaved for less weight and better clearances. Roof windows or clerestories improved lighting and ventilation and became a fixed feature of streetcars for many generations. By the mid-1860s, the clerestory ran the full length of the car body. Stephenson came to call this the Bombay roof, presumably because it was first used on cars built for that city."

---

1. White, John. *Horsecars, Cable Cars and Omnibuses,* Dover Publishers, 1974.

Figure 1: An example of a mule car with clerestory windows, at St. Louis (Mills) and Stanton Streets with the O.T. Bassett Lumber Company in the background. It appears to be heading west toward downtown.

Stephenson was to become the builder of El Paso's first mule car, No. 1, sometime before 1882. Since No.1 was not fitted with clerestory upper windows for light and ventilation, it is safe to assume it arrived in El Paso as a previously-owned vehicle and may date back as far as the 1860s.

The history of the mule-powered streetcar system in El Paso has been largely over-simplified by historians in the past. There is the pastoral semblance of Mandy the Mule ambling down a dusty street with car No. 1, the implication being that these two were the sum total of the animal-powered street railway of the 1880s and 1890s. The truth is that there were up to four companies competing at various times with confusing, sometimes interlocking, sets of El Paso movers and shakers serving as officers and board members. In addition, rather than one mule and one car, there were more than 13 cars and 40 mules.

By the end of the 1870s, just before the arrival of the railroads and a growth explosion, El Paso already had newspapers, and within a couple of years would have banks and a railroad. About that time, there began to be talk about the need for a public transit system. El Paso had been incorporated by the Texas legislature as a city on May 17, 1873, and immediately plunged into partisan politics, Ben Dowell being elected the first mayor.

Owen P. White[2] related the story of Colonel James Marr's arrival in El Paso in 1878. Col. Marr established a transfer and hack business and also operated a ferry boat over the Rio Grande. However, this enterprise was still not adequate to satisfy the transportation needs of the growing community. A street railway was needed for more efficient and reliable public transportation. Street railways at that time almost always consisted of small streetcars on rails, drawn by horses or mules. Colonel Marr would later become one of the contractors in the building of the street railways.

El Paso had its fourth election in 1881 and Joseph Magoffin was elected mayor. For some time, Magoffin and his business partners had been considering the installation of a street railway and now they felt the time was right. On January 14th, 1881, the city awarded a franchise to the El Paso Street Railway Company and its first officers, Joseph Magoffin, J.H. Harrison, George W. Thomas, J.R. Currie, C.B. Wilson, and J.P. Hague. The company was given the right to lay tracks in city streets and to operate a mule car system. A second franchise was awarded on August 30, 1881, to the City Railway Company of El Paso, backed by Samuel Schutz, J.M. Thatcher, J.H. Bates, William Kellar, Andrew Kellar, H.R. Brickerhoff, and M. Samaniego. This franchise also included the exclusive authority to build a bridge across the Rio Grande.

A controversy arose immediately, since the mayor, Joseph Magoffin, had an interest in the first company, the El Paso Street Railway. No one seemed overly concerned about a conflict of interest as Mayor Magoffin did everything he could to block the second company's franchise. His objections were that the franchise gave operation rights over streets which were not yet deeded to the city. He felt it was not within the power of the city to authorize the building of an international bridge. In addition, the franchise gave the new company the power to build switches, turntables, and sidings where they wished on city streets. Magoffin's contention was that this, at the very least, could interfere with traffic. The mayor's petition to deny the franchise failed for lack of votes and the franchise was granted.

2. White, Owen P. *Out of the Desert,* McMath Printers, 1924.

In those days, it did not seem terribly difficult to obtain a franchise if you had enough votes on the city council. Although franchises were granted to various companies, the difficult task of raising money and attracting investors had to be addressed before construction could begin.

The editor of the *Lone Star*[3] newspaper, in his editorial, approved the granting of a franchise to the City Railway Company and reasoned that two companies would be beneficial to the city by stimulating competition. It should be noted here that, although articles of incorporation are filed and franchises granted, they only give the legal right to build, and do not *encumber* the group or company to build, although they might lose that right if they did not build.

In a newspaper article of October 1881[4], it was noted that a proviso had been added to the City Railway franchise (the Schutz group), which required the company to begin building on El Paso Street, providing the first company (El Paso Street Railway, Magoffin, et al) had not already done so. El Paso Street had always been a strong commercial street and the business owners may have been exercising their political clout by requiring one or the other of the companies to build on El Paso Street.

Newspaper editors continued to push for a streetcar system, and in January 1882[5], editorialized that since about six hundred people crossed the Rio Grande daily to Paso del Norte (later to become Ciudad Juarez) at that time, the number could be increased significantly if there were a streetcar in operation. In answer to critics that the line could not pay for itself, it was noted that 600 passengers paying ten cents each would be sixty dollars per day or $21,900 a year. That would offset the predicted cost of $10,000 to $15,000 for constructing and stocking the line.

In an article in the newspaper in January 1882[6], Captain J.A. Bates of the City Railway Company indicated that a contract for grading had been let and that a design for an international bridge had been accepted by the company, an indication that bridge construction would begin soon. He somewhat optimistically predicted El Paso citizens might be able to ride a streetcar across the river within 60 days.

---

3. *The Lone Star,* Nov. 16, 1881.
4. *ibid,* Oct. 19, 1881.
5. *The Lone Star,* Jan. 25, 1882
6. *ibid.,* Jan. 29, 1882,

The Charter of the El Paso Street Railway and Bridge Company[7] was written and filed in the Department of State of Texas on February 25, 1881. The charter indicated the purpose was: "the building, equipment, maintenance, and management of street railways in and through the streets of the city of El Paso, Texas and the building, maintaining, and management of a bridge of wood or iron across the Rio Grande River between the cities of El Paso, Texas and El Paso del Norte, Mexico for the crossing of a street railway and all kinds of vehicles, animals and horse or foot passengers."

The differences between the two groups apparently were soon reconciled as the minutes[8] of the May 6, 1882, meeting of the Board of Directors of the El Paso Street Railway indicate that directors Solomon Schutz, J.F. Crosby, Joseph Magoffin, A, Krakauer, and Noyes Rand were present. Schutz was elected President, Rand Vice-President, and Bates Secretary and Superintendent. Rand and Magoffin were elected to act as an Executive Committee with Schutz in dealings with the Street Railway of Paso del Norte, Mexico, their across-river counterpart. By the spring of 1882, it would appear the two groups were combined for all practical purposes and money for construction was being raised.

---

7. Copy of the original charter in the author's possession, from the collection of Patrick Rand.
8. Copy of the original minutes in the author's possession via the Rand Collection.

Figure 2: No. 5, a Brill car.

Who then, could be credited with actually building the first mule car line to Paso del Norte across the bridge?

Even Owen P. White, in the year 1924, declined to enter this controversy. He reasoned:

> "There are numerous individuals still living in El Paso who claim the honor and distinction of being personally responsible for the inauguration of high class and elegant streetcar service, which El Pasoans enjoyed between 1882 and 1905" (Ed. note: actually 1882–1902). He continues: "To us, however, the identity of the individual who originated the idea of furnishing El Paso with mule car transportation is not of absorbing interest." (Ed. note: Quite probably, he simply did not know). "Most of the old timers had something to do with it. We are not going to engender any jealousies at this late date by giving Crosby, Magoffin, or Mills any preference over Zach White or Samuel Schutz."

The preponderance of the evidence, however, is that Magoffin, Schutz, Rand, Krakauer, and Crosby were primarily responsible. Anson Mills was not even in the picture at this time. One individual who has never received due credit was

Noyes Rand. He is seldom mentioned in writings of historians, yet he was Vice President, a Board member, on the Executive Committee, and was the largest stockholder in the El Paso Street Railway during the most crucial planning and building stages.

The exigencies of building a street railway are illustrated in the minutes[9] of the El Paso Street Railway when a resolution was drafted and approved to levy a 5% assessment on capital stockholders for the purpose of paying for the iron for said railway, as well as freight and other charges for materials already arriving. An additional 3% assessment was levied upon the capital stock for the purpose of paying for lumber, freight and associated charges in building the new bridge. Noyes Rand, having the largest amount of stock ($13,888), paid $694 and $416, respectively, on the assessments. Schutz, owning $11,500 in stock, paid $575 and $345. Other major stockholders included J.H. Bates at $11,000, and G.B. Zimpleman, J.M. Thatcher, J.F. Crosby, and W.R. Bates, all at $10,000. There were a number of lesser stockholders including Hague, Harrison, Fewel, Krakauer, and Judge Magoffin at $6,944 each. At that same meeting, the routing of the first line was changed from Utah (later Mesa) to go south on El Paso Street, east on Fifth Street (later on Seventh), and south on Stanton to the river. It is interesting to note that in the later 1894 consolidation of the companies, Anson Mills was the major shareholder with 361 shares, and that Judge Magoffin's participation had been reduced to only two shares.

Expenses obviously continued to rise as new assessments on capital stock were made in the amounts of 5% in September and 10% in November of 1882.

In October 1882, it was reported in the *El Paso Herald*[10] that the "long talked about" streetcars had arrived and would be ready in a few days. Four or five cars had been received, and the editor congratulated Mssrs. Schutz, Bates and Rand.

---

9. Copy of the minutes of the Director's meeting of the El Paso Street Railway of June 12, 1882, in the author's possession, from the Rand Collection.
10. *El Paso Herald*, October 11, 1882.

The Line to Paso del Norte (Cd. Juarez)

An article in the *Herald*[1] extolled the opening of the line to Paso del Norte "with the pomp that was due such an important achievement." J. Ochoa, the President of the Bridge and City Railway of Paso del Norte, was one of the speakers as two cars, adorned with flags of the two nations, waited in the center of the bridge to transport VIP's to a celebratory feast. Mr. Schutz spoke on behalf of the Americans. The line and bridge were opened for streetcar traffic in October 1882, and for other vehicular traffic in January 1883.

A different type of historical confusion is revealed as newspapers[2] reported the opening of new bridge construction in November 1884 by the City Street Railway. The wording of the article seems to give the clue. This is likely a new bridge to replace the 1882 Stanton Street Bridge swept away in the flood of June, 1884. For example, in Lewis Cumming's *Zach White, Pioneer Capitalist*[3], he states that: "even so, it was not until August 1884, that the contract for the construction of the El Paso portion of the international bridge was granted." The newspaper[4] reported that the first trip across the river had taken place in October, 1882. Again, in December 1882, the *Lone Star*[5] reported that streetcars "now run regularly from this city to Paso del Norte." One problem in researching the lines and the bridges is that historians and writers have often assumed that franchises granted equals lines and bridges built, but that was not always the case.

---

1. *Ibid*, January 10, 1883.
2. *Ibid, Nov. 8, 1884.*
3. Cummings, Lewis, *Zach White, Pioneer Capitalist*, thesis, 1969, El Paso Public Library.
4. *The Lone Star*, Oct. 7, 1882.
5. *Ibid*, December 21, 1882.

Figure 3: only known photo of a City Street Railway mule car, location not known, with railroad cars in the background.

One of the problems of constructing any new international bridge was getting permission from all governments involved—city, state, and federal. La Compania de Ferrocarriles Urbanos Y Puente was to start construction from the Mexican shore and tie in with the bridge extension from the American side. It was necessary to obtain permission from various local, state, and federal Mexican agencies.

The first streetcars originally ran down El Paso Street to Fifth Street (later on Seventh), then over to Stanton, going over the Stanton Street Bridge and entering Juarez by way of Avenida Lerdo. The terminal was at the intersection of this avenue with Comercio Street. This was one line and was all prior to the construction of the Santa Fe Street Bridge. By 1883, the Pierson Hotel was advertising trolley service from the Southern Pacific train station on Kansas Street all the way to the Mexican Central depot in Juarez.

The San Antonio Street Line

The second line, constructed later, ran out Magoffin Avenue to Judge Magoffin's home. The construction of the San Antonio line in November 1883, gave employment to 24 individuals and six teams. On the 12th of December, two new cars were received from the Brill Car Works in Philadelphia for this line.

Figure 4: This mule car, not No.1, is at the end of the San Antonio Street line near El Paso Street. The old County Courthouse is in the background. The driver will now unhitch the mule and walk him around to the other end to go back in the opposite direction.

The photograph above shows a mule car on San Antonio at the end of the line at the intersection of El Paso Street. It can be seen that the track ends and does not connect with the line on El Paso Street. This had always puzzled this author, since it was assumed they were two lines of the same company. It appears, however, that the two lines were operated independently, at least initially.

From the recollections of E.A. Shelton[1]: "I arrived in El Paso, February 6, 1886. The city was fortunate in having gas, electric lights, telephone and water works; the latter, however, not very satisfactory. Many water wagons ran between El Paso and Deming, New Mexico, and water was sold on the street for drinking purposes, and many used this. [The water was shipped by rail to El Paso and placed on wagons for distribution.] We did not have any sewerage or paved streets and but a few paved sidewalks, and these were paved with tar and gravel…The main business street was El Paso Street from Mills and San Francisco Streets on the north to First or Second Streets on the south. There were a few stores on San Antonio, but not many east of Mesa at that time."

Figure 5: A longer view of San Antonio Street looking east with a mule car traveling toward the camera.

The San Antonio Street line first operated out San Antonio to Magoffin, then on Magoffin almost to Cotton Street, the end of the line. As late as 1894, the line was extended farther down San Antonio, new stables were constructed at San Antonio and Cotton, and the loop was completed over Cotton Street. Now cars could go out San Antonio and return via Magoffin in a loop. Another advantage

---

1. *El Paso Merchant and Civic Leader, Samuel J. Freudenthal*, p.42, Southwestern Studies Monograph No. 11, Texas Western Press, 1965.

of this arrangement was that it served the Texas and Pacific Railroad station. The extension of the San Antonio Street line, which had been requested in 1889, also gave service to the Fairgrounds in the Cotton Street area, which often hosted circuses and horse racing.

Figure 6: Completing the loop at Magoffin and San Antonio Streets, the mule car is about to merge with the San Antonio Street tracks, and will head west to downtown. In the background is the original First Baptist Church, on the site of the present Toltec Building. The gentleman on the bicycle is S.H. Newman, editor of the newspaper, the *Lone Star*.

After a few years of operation, there were some complaints and some grumbling about service. For example, in 1885, it was reported that passengers were being charged a double fare after seven-thirty in the evening, plus a fee to be paid to the driver. About this time, due to lack of maintenance and water runoff, the tracks in the middle of San Antonio Street were, in places, one to two feet higher than the surrounding street, making its use by other vehicles difficult. A newspaper editor also complained that it was poor practice for the streetcar company not to have a car waiting by the Opera House at the close of a performance, even though the last scheduled run was at 9 p.m.

In the early days, Oregon Street was not cut through between San Antonio and Mills. However, after that was done, the San Antonio mule car made a loop up Oregon past the Federal Courthouse and the Sheldon Hotel, then through Little Plaza (later Pioneer) down El Paso Street to San Antonio Street.

Figure 7: No. 7, with a clerestory roof, in Cuidad Juarez.

The El Paso Street Railway built a line on Crosby Avenue, later St. Louis Street (now Mills), connecting the Southern Pacific depot on Kansas to Little Plaza. After several years, another line went south on Stanton from St. Louis, straight to the Stanton Street Bridge.

The Belt Line on the American Side

Traffic congestion on the Juarez line was reported in 1888, as the same route was used for cars going in both directions. Therefore, it was often necessary for one car to wait at a switch on one side of the bridge for the car going in the opposite direction to pass. The situation inconvenienced and irritated paying passengers, however, the problem was largely rectified in December 1888 by the construction of a belt line. Although there was still only one bridge in operation, there was constructed a loop on the American side so that cars went in one direction and did not have to pass each other. The loop extended from the bridge south on Stanton, west on Seventh, north on El Paso, east on St. Louis, and south again on Stanton. The Stanton Street extension had been long lobbied for by Stanton Street merchants[1]. In fact, they had raised a fund by subscription to begin grading the line. The track had been laid for three months, but the connections had not been made and no cars had run on the line. A committee of merchants visited all of the members of the Board of Directors of the street railway that they could find and got commitments for the Stanton line to be put in operation as soon as possible. The superintendent of the line noted that he was contemplating putting two more cars in operation as soon as the belt line was connected, making eight in all. The new schedule would allow the run from the Mexican Central depot in Juarez to the El Paso Post Office to be made in 25 minutes.

---

1. *El Paso Times,* July 22, 1888.

Figure 8: Stanton Street Bridge with mule car tracks looking north from the Mexican side.

In 1887, Samuel Schutz applied for a new franchise for a company to be called the Santa Fe Street Railway. He had gone straight to the United States government for a franchise and obtained it. In 1888, he received a telegram from Washington telling him the bill he had sought for permission to build a bridge across the Rio Grande had become law and he could begin building. When interviewed[2], Schutz stated that he was awaiting the return of Mr. Felipe Arrellano from Mexico City with permission from the Mexican authorities to build the line in Paso del Norte (Cd. Juarez) and the new bridge. Schutz indicated that Arrellano and his partners would be major shareholders in the new company on the Mexican side. He had wanted to build a bridge at the end of Santa Fe Street where a small ferry had previously operated. He appeared before the city council and was able to obtain a city franchise with the cooperation of the city fathers who also were interested in having a bridge on Santa Fe Street. The new line would start from the Little Plaza, run down San Francisco Street to Santa Fe Street, then south to the river. Once the Santa Fe Street Bridge was constructed and the Mexican portion built, it would meet the Magoffin group's line at Lerdo and Comercio, thence by the Customs House and down Juarez Avenue to the new bridge.

---

2. *El Paso Times,* August 28, 1888.

Schutz continued by saying that, on a recent trip to the East Coast, he had ordered six passenger cars for the line that will run across the river. He indicated he would have them shipped as soon as the line was prepared for them. On the same trip, he contracted for the iron for the rails. Schutz also commented that the cars would be of the newest types, fitted with a mirror allowing the driver to be able to see into the car without turning around. They would also be fitted with an apparatus that would allow the driver to open the door on the rear platform while still at his post on the front platform.

By October 1888, a survey of the new line had been made by City Engineer, F. Ashton. Schutz indicated he had been ready for a month to begin the project, but had been delayed pending the return of Mr. Arrellano from Mexico City.

Enter Zach White

Writers and historians are in fundamental agreement as to the circumstances of Zach White's arrival. He was another El Paso pioneer who came to the city shortly before the arrival of the railroads. At the time, the Southern Pacific was operating a passenger line from San Francisco through Los Angeles and as far as Tucson. From the latter place, the line was being built east toward El Paso. At the time Mr. White decided to make El Paso his permanent home, the end of line was about 20 miles west of El Paso. He completed his journey in a stagecoach.

A little hardware store on South El Paso Street was Zach White's first business in the city. A few doors north on the same street was a grocery store for which he had furnished the money. An astute businessman, Zach White prospered[1] and invested in Schutz's streetcar company. He was an active member of the firm, and as such, engineered the plans which resulted in the construction of the Santa Fe Street Bridge.

Zach White was already on board when Schutz made his pitch to the City Council for a franchise in July of 1888. In an interesting aspect of the wording of the request for the franchise, the owners of the Santa Fe Street Railway asked for permission to haul freight on their mule car line. The ordinance passed without much discussion and only later did the public become somewhat alarmed at the possibility of heavy freight moving through the main streets of the city. Some citizens wondered aloud whether a steam engine might be brought in, thereby creating a safety and noise nuisance on the street. White and Schutz tried to calm fears, indicating that freight cars would not be any longer than a regular streetcar, would be mule-powered, and would probably only be allowed to run at nighttime. There is, however, no evidence that this scheme was ever implemented.

The story of Zach White's building of the Santa Fe Street Bridge and causing the widening of Avenida Juarez to accommodate a mule car line is told in several places, including Henry Leinbach's[2] treatise on the streetcar system, by Owen White, by Lewis Cummings[3] and others. The basic information is traced back to

---

1. Assessed value of Zach White's worth increased from $1,538 in 1882 to $370,660 in 1887.

a September 8, 1921 article in the *El Paso Times*, the substance of which is told here. As part of his intention to build a Santa Fe Street bridge and extend his carline into Cd. Juarez by way of Avenida Juarez, Zach White realized that the street on the Mexican side would need to have a seventy foot right of way, but was told by the Mayor that the city could not reimburse the locals for their losses if their houses, which encroached on the right of way, were torn down. White reportedly took the Mayor of Juarez up on the roof of the Customs House and pointed out what he needed. White told the mayor that he would personally reimburse the owners for their houses, and it is said the street was cleared within 48 hours. This impressed the Juarez mayor as being beneficial to the business owners of his city, as well. The unfortunate dwellers on the avenue were subsequently evicted, and supposedly paid for their property. Grading and work on the new line commenced immediately thereafter. This was a definite victory for the new carline as the route into Paso del Norte (Cd. Juarez) would be more direct than the existing line.

Since the Santa Fe Street Railway would need to cross the Santa Fe Railroad, Schutz and White opted for a flagman to protect the safety of the crossing. The new Santa Fe Street Bridge was open to pedestrian traffic by June 1, 1889, and it was estimated that streetcars would be crossing in about two weeks. On that day, 200 people crossed the free bridge between the hours of 10 a.m. and 2 p.m.

---

2. Leinbach, Henry. *The El Paso Electric Company, Transportation Division, A Tentative History*, Southern Traction Annals, 1976.
3. Cummings, Lewis, *Zach White, Pioneer Capitalist*, thesis in the El Paso Public Library, 1969.

Anson Mills and the Consolidation of the Mule Car Companies

In another unresolved conflict with previously published accounts, it was widely reported that Anson Mills was an early investor and partner with Joseph Magoffin in the first street railway between El Paso and Ciudad Juarez.

In an article entitled "General Mills Saves the Situation", from the *El Paso Times*[1], it was noted that the question of a transit system and the organization of a mule car line had become a topic of discussion. The article states that General Anson Mills, who laid the town off in 1859, came to the rescue. "With United States Senator Bates, of Tennessee, and Judge Joseph Magoffin, he organized a streetcar company, and by 1882, the cars were in operation." This oft-repeated assertion is not supported by documentary evidence. In 1882, Mills was still serving in the U.S. Army and was stationed, at the time, at Fort Davis, Texas. Although it is known he had some business interests in El Paso at the time, he is not listed either as an incorporator, a director, or an investor in the original company. Unless he was a very silent partner, which is highly unlikely considering his character, it appears that Anson Mills was not involved until the early 1890s, when he became an investor in the combined transit companies. The myth of Anson Mill's participation in the first street railway continued into modern times. In an El Paso Electric Company publication[2], there is the assertion: "Seeing the need for more adequate local transportation facilities, a group of men headed by General Anson Mills, who laid out the streets and designed the Mills Building, obtained a charter of the El Paso Street Railway Company and the privilege of operating a mule-drawn streetcar system."

---

1. *El Paso Times,* September 8, 1921.
2. *E News, From Mule Car to Nuclear Power,* El Paso Electric Company, 1991.

Anson Mills[3] relates his version of events of the 1890s:

> "When the Santa Fe, Mexican Central, Texas & Pacific, and Sunset Routes were completed to El Paso, about 1880, the five thousand people of El Paso, and eight thousand of Juarez, organized four street railways, two in El Paso (one on El Paso Street and one on Santa Fe Street), connecting with the two similar Mexican roads on the Juarez side at the middle of the Stanton and Juarez Street bridges. Stock in these roads was subscribed in the East, but each road had a president, four directors and other officers. All of whom, to be popular with the public, made deadheads of the officials of the two cities, policemen, collectors of customs, revenue officers, and so forth. There was, therefore, great maintenance expense and little revenue to the stockholders, and the equipment soon degenerated into a most impoverished condition. When it became necessary to assess stockholders or go into bankruptcy, Senator Bates, from Tennessee, a personal friend, complained to me that he and his wife had twenty-five thousands dollars in stock of the El Paso street road. He was unable to pay his assessment and, as El Paso was said to be my town, he thought I ought to do something to relieve him. We went to El Paso and he had some stormy interviews with the managers of his road. Suggesting the possibility of the consolidation of the four roads, I told him that, as I had confidence of the Mexicans as well as the Americans of the two cities, if he was willing to come with me, we might encourage the stockholders in New York to give proxies for a majority of the stock.
>
> We saw the principal stockholders in New York, one of them a cousin of J.P. Morgan, obtained proxies for a majority of the stock, and power of attorney to represent the stockholders in the consolidation of the four roads. The El Paso Street road was advertised for sale under foreclosure. Authorized by its stockholders to purchase, I did so, and then obtained from the Mexican stockholders and others in El Paso, proxies for a majority of the stock in the other roads. Calling a meeting of each of the four roads, I proposed a consolidation into one company, making the circuit through both cities, to be styled the El Paso and Juarez Traction Company, with charters from the states of Texas and Chihuahua. Governor Ahumanda and the Governor of Texas both granted charters. The four companies made a statement of their financial condition and expressed willingness to merge in the new international company. It had a capital of two hundred thousand dollars, distributed to each company in proportion to their annual gains in the past five years. The directors of the four companies elected officers for the new company. Messrs. Z.T. White, Joseph Magoffin, J. A. Happer, Max Weber, and I were elected directors, and by them I was elected president. There was some disagreement as to the stock to be allotted to the Santa Fe Street Company, and the officers to be elected, so Messrs. White, Maxon, and Gordon declined to enter the consolidation. It

---

3. Mills, Anson, *My Story*, 1921.

was agreed to run the roads jointly, but the Santa Fe Company kept its own organization. The four companies were run as one road, all deadheads were canceled and the company soon prospered."

Mills, in other words, participated in the reorganization and consolidation of the mule car companies in the 1890s, but he does not claim to be one of the first organizers in 1882. Most autobiographical accounts tend to be somewhat self-serving by nature and Anson Mills' is no exception. This is not to diminish his considerable accomplishments, but rather to put them in their proper context. Mills had been an early El Paso pioneer, but had sided with the Union at the outbreak of the Civil War and left before the city was occupied by the Confederates. He rose in the Union Army to the rank of General and returned many years later to head the International Water and Boundary Commission. When he approached the problem of the several mule car companies, his perspective was that of the consummate businessman who wanted a system that was efficient and practical. He felt the companies had been run in such a manner as to accommodate the owners and not the public and that the various companies were top-heavy in administration. That his ideas collided with those of Zach White was perhaps inevitable. From Lewis Cummings' work on Zach White is the other version:

> "There were serious differences between Zach White and Anson Mills on basic policies concerning the merger. For obvious reasons, White wanted to convert the system to electric cars while Mills insisted on retaining the old mule car system. Being a large stockholder and member of the directory of the El Paso Gas, Electric Light and Power Company, Zach White offered to supply the electric power at cost. This would have been to the very great advantage of the electric company and particularly in view of the difficulties that were arising because of the White company's loss of business to the International Light and Power Company. Not surprisingly, Anson Mills insisted that the combined company would be in the power of Mills and his directors, and the cost of electricity would be raised at any time they felt so inclined. In addition, it would cost $20,000 to install the electric system and $10,000 a year to operate it. This he (Anson Mills) felt would only add to the cost of the existing operation which would function well under the current system. Mills, with an eye towards economy, also wished to shorten the streetcar system by about 2 and 2/3 miles by eliminating the Santa Fe Street line. This, of course, was strenuously opposed by Zack White.
>
> Because of this impasse, still another company was proposed on November 8, 1900, known as the El Paso and Juarez Traction Company, in hopes of combining the four companies and resolving the differences between White

and Mills. But now consolidation of the four lines was tied up because of Mexican politics. Felipe Seijas, the lawyer for the Mexican lines, said an additional $2,910 was needed for seals and fees. At first Mills, acting as the directing force behind the consolidation, refused to pay[4]. Later he requested, and was granted, funds from the four companies for this purpose, and the consolidation was approved by Governor Ahumada of Chihuahua. On the 13th of November 1900, Mills called a meeting to complete the consolidation proceedings. At that time, Zach White submitted a telegram from J.J. Gordon, holder of 148 shares in the Santa Fe Street line, stating: 'I authorize you to sign deeds from Santa Fe Company to Traction Company providing they are going to change to electricity...' He also submitted a wire from J. H. Maxon, holder of fifty shares. 'Routes have been selected', it said.

'Make no transfer. When they have bridge and road equally ours is plenty of time'. Both Maxon and Gordon were, in addition to being stockholders in the railroad company, holders of stock in the electric company, and were interested in furthering the electric business. After reading the two wires, White also stated his objection to the merger and left the meeting. After White's departure, the meeting continued, and the consolidation of the El Paso Street Railway, La Compania del Ferrocarril Urbano y Puente and la Compania de Ferrocariles Urbanos de Ciudad Juarez was accomplished."

Figure 9: No. 5 in Pioneer Plaza by the Plaza Block Building. Note the muddy street and the driver's heavy coat.

---

4. *El Paso Daily Herald*, Nov. 8, 1900.

Nevertheless, public opinion was becoming aroused over the state of the transportation system in El Paso. The *El Paso Daily Herald* [5] protested the antiquidated mule car systems and deplored the fact that the local streetcars were as far from the 20th century as ever. Eastern capital would not come to El Paso since the existing companies had the rights to bridges and the use of the public streets tied up. The *Daily Herald* also claimed that when the Eastern capital heard that the El Paso and Juarez Traction Company alone wanted $200,000 for its franchise, it lost interest in local investments. Although the actual amount was unstated, the additional cost of purchasing the franchise and equipment of the Santa Fe and Juarez Street Railway Companies would have made the purchase of the El Paso transportation systems prohibitive.

---

5. *El Paso Daily Herald,* Jan. 26, 1901.

The Clamor for Electric Cars by 1900

In 1901 there was some discussion that the consolidated railway companies would try to get electric power from the local electric company and thus convert to electric streetcars, but it was believed that the electric company was already overtaxed and probably would be unable to supply the necessary current. Anson Mills[1] publicly stated that "If Zach White will behave himself and furnish power for less than the cost of mules; we will convert to an electric system."

In spite of the previous loss of interest in El Paso streetcar companies by some East Coast investors, several Eastern groups were interested in obtaining control of the local transportation system. E.W.Davis, of Pittsburgh, represented one such group, and D.M. Goodrich represented the Stone & Webster Company of Boston. Rumors persisted concerning the intentions of the El Paso financial community. Felix Martinez, President of the International Light and Power Company, was accused by Captain Juan S. Hart of acting in bad faith toward representatives of the capitalists. Hart accused him of negotiating with Davis before Goodrich had ample opportunity to make an offer for the purchase of the International Light & Power Company, which would be needed for the operation of the street railway system if the Goodrich people were able to obtain the franchise and convert to electricity. Martinez denied showing any favoritism, and further denied the rumor that he had approached Zach White about any options connected with his electric or railway companies[2].

While confusion continued over the possibility of outside capital coming to El Paso, the managers of the consolidated company announced it had ordered a new bridge to be built across the river, and new electric cars had been ordered for their line. The cars were to be delivered in El Paso about May 1, 1901. The change in type of transportation was to apply to Santa Fe Street only, and if the plan were satisfactory, it would extend to the rest of the line later[3]. No evidence of concrete

---

1. *Ibid.*
2. *ibid,* April 10, 1901.

action was shown, however, and it is probable that their move was designed to force the hand of one of the outside groups. Improved facilities on the part of one of the existing companies would undoubtedly increase the selling cost and confuse the issue even further.

The idea that to electrify the trolley system would only necessitate the stringing of overhead wire was quite naive. The electric cars were much heavier than mule cars and could not ride on the same light rail and ungraded right of way. The capital cost of an electric system would include new street grading, new and heavier rails laid, the overhead trolley wire system with poles, the purchase of the new cars, and quite likely, a new carbarn to house and maintain them. Although there would be no need for stables for the mules, there would be a significant need for machine shops, electrical shops, motor rebuilding and overhead line maintenance. The streetcars would be heavier and faster and would require a much-improved track and right of way.

Meanwhile, the group headed by D.M. Goodrich of Cambridge, Massachusetts, was granted a franchise to construct and operate an electric car line in El Paso and to operate under the name of the El Paso Electric Railway Company. It is interesting that none of the franchises granted for either mule or electric companies appeared to be exclusive. The fact that one company held a franchise did not appear to deter other companies from seeking a similar franchise.

A bond of $5,000 was posted guaranteeing construction of the six miles of track[4] by the El Paso Electric Railway. To show his faith in the new company, D. M. Goodrich shortly thereafter petitioned the city council and received permission to shorten the time requirement for construction of his line from six months to three months[5]. Next, to show his firm meant business, he petitioned the county commissioners, asking for a franchise to use county roads for a period of fifty years for his electric line. This petition was approved, and the commissioners granted the franchise without a dissenting vote[6]. The news of this faith in expansion did cause something of a renewed interest in property along the proposed county road routes.

While the Goodrich group negotiated for their franchise, Mr. Davis stated that his party held an option on the old streetcar company and expected to negotiate its purchase shortly. He also stated that he had an option on the International Light & Power Company[7]. However, he failed to follow it through to

---

3. *Ibid*, April 12, 1901.
4. *Ibid.*, April 24, 1901.
5. *ibid*, April 26, 1901.
6. *Ibid.* May 4, 1901.

conclusion and the option he held on the Santa Fe Street Railway Company expired while he was out of El Paso. Later, he was too ill to return. When he did meet with Zach White and the other members of the old company board, he found they were asking $25,000 more than they had before the option expired. Davis received a second blow when he found his option on the International Power and Light Company had also expired. The company refused to grant any other long-term options, but would sell to anyone who could make a good offer[8].

It would seem to the casual observer that, at this particular time in El Paso history, the more valuable commodity was the electric power and not necessarily the street railway franchise.

Speculation as to the fate of the old railway company continued through the summer, and a local newspaper made an announcement on October 25, 1901, that seemed to deny a prediction made by the *Herald* a month earlier. It stated that the El Paso and Juarez Traction Company had been purchasing a large number of mules and had about fifty-six at that time. An employee of the railway company claimed that the purchase of the mules was only to cover the needs of the winter, when traffic was heaviest. Still another rumor circulated that Zach White had gone east to purchase the necessary equipment to transform his line to an electric car line[9].

While El Pasoans pondered the fate of the old mule car companies, Goodrich's El Paso Electric Railway Company was busily building. The people of El Paso hoped the electric line to Juarez would be completed by January 1902, since the Winter Carnival was to be held then, and many people from out of the city would be present. Indeed, chances for the completion of the electric line looked good, and the El Paso Electric Railway Company was already selling advertising space on the back of transfer tickets[10].

One problem faced by the new company was the lack of permission from Juarez officials to repair the Stanton Street Bridge. They finally appealed to Zach White's Santa Fe Street Company and received permission to use the Santa Fe Street Bridge. This is most likely the origin of the traditional return routing of the Juarez line, i.e., north across the Santa Fe Street Bridge, north on Santa Fe, jog east on Chamizal Court, then continuing north on El Paso Street to downtown. Both firms stressed the fact that this did not mean merger, in spite of the cooperative arrangement[11].

---

7. *Ibid,* April 14, 1901.
8. *Ibid.,* May 17, 1901.
9. *El Paso Times,* November 30, 1901.
10. *El Paso Daily Herald,* December 7, 1901.

On the 27th of December, Goodrich's new company proudly announced that eight motor cars and four trailers had been shipped from the St. Louis Car Company and could be in operation on the Juarez run by the date set for the Winter Carnival. Cars would carry a crew of two, a motorman and a conductor, a standard practice in the street railway industry at that time. El Paso Electric Railway, however, preferred to call them *trainmen*.

---

11. *El Paso Daily Herald*, December 13, 1901.

Recollections of a former St. Louis Newspaper Man

The following El Paso sketches were written by a former St. Louis newsman and were published in the early part of the century[1].

> "*The St Louis of the Southwest.* That is the name I have heard applied to El Paso since my arrival here ten days ago. Six years ago, I visited El Paso and I am amazed at the wonderful growth it has had and all the rapid advancement it has made in all those respects which pertain to a higher form of civilization since that time. Six years ago the street car system of El Paso consisted of four or five dinky cars, each one drawn by a decrepit mule. Of these mules the hero, the patriarch, the town pet, was Mandy.
>
> Fifteen years ago the street car service of El Paso consisted of one car, one driver, and one mule, and that one mule was 'Mandy'. (Ed. note: this would be about 1890 and is factually incorrect as there were a number of cars and mules by that time). She had been a veteran of the San Antonio street car system. She slaved for that people until she was thought to have outlived her usefulness. Then, between fifteen and sixteen years ago, she was brought to El Paso to perform the easier task of hauling the sole street car of this village.

---

1. Author unknown, *St. Louis Star*, 1905.

Figure 10: Mandy and No. 1 on Cotton Street.

From that time there never was a day when Mandy failed to drag the car throughout the weary route around and about El Paso until the present (1905) superb electric car system was installed three years ago the eleventh day of this month. During those twelve years or so of local streetcar servitude, Mandy came to be the best known and most popular object in El Paso It was no uncommon sight to see women stop Mandy on the street and feed her a handful of daisies. Children used to play tag under Mandy and around her legs and fearlessly pull her tail.

Mandy had the reputation of being able to walk slower than retributive justice after a wealthy criminal, and could trot slower than any other mule could walk. Long after the present generation has passed away Mandy's name will be spoken daily in El Paso homes. One frequently hears such expressions as 'so and so is as good natured as Mandy', or 'that boy is slower than Mandy', 'I have waited as patiently as Mandy', etc.

It was my fortune, when in El Paso six years ago, to ride in a car drawn by Mandy. I shall not say how slow we traveled, because if did, I would not be believed. After riding and waiting, principally waiting, for an hour or two, Mandy came to a dead halt in the middle of a block and, to all appearances, went to sleep. The driver urged her in soporific tones to proceed, and finally he shook the lines gently. Still there was nothing doing. Mandy slept. The driver calmly resigned himself to the inevitable, sat down on his stool, rolled a cigarette, and placidly smoked.

Losing patience, I accosted him. 'Why don't you make that mule go?' I asked. 'Cos it ain't in a goin' humor', he answered serenely. 'Why don't you whip it?' 'Ain't got no whip', he answered, beginning to look sullen. 'But there are lots of loose rocks on the street', I persisted. 'Pick up some of them and pelt him with them.' The driver rose from his stool, threw away his cigarette stub and eyed me scornfully. 'Stranger', he said, 'that mule is Mandy. If I should hit Mandy, I would be shot before I had time to draw another breath.

He's a privileged character—that old white mule is the adopted child of this town.' Then he rolled another cigarette, touched me for a match and resumed his smoke. I left the car and walked the remainder of the distance.

The streetcar in use in El Paso was a little bob-tailed affair which, with judicious squeezing, would hold eight persons, provided none were very fleshy. The rails were thin strips of iron or tin. About half the time the wheels would run on the rails. The rest of the time, they would bump over the cobblestones. The cars seemed to bump and teeter and clatter fully one way as much as they did the other.

J.A. Eddy told me a good story about the old time El Paso Street Railway. 'The mule cars used to pass our home', said Mr. Eddy. 'I remember one day about four years ago, I decided to go downtown. My wife looked and saw a car coming. As was customary, she sent our little girl out to tell the driver that I wished to go downtown, but was not then ready to start. A few minutes later, I changed my notion and decided that I would stay at home that day. Sometime afterward, I do not know whether it was ten minutes or half and hour later, I noticed the car standing in front of the house. I asked my wife if she was intending to order something from downtown, and she said: 'Oh, I forgot I had the car stopped to wait for you.' Then she sent our girl out to tell the driver that Papa had decided not to go downtown and he need not wait any longer. We never thought of there being anything strange about such occurrences in those days. The interval between cars was so great that no one hesitated to ask the driver to wait while he or she got ready. If a woman downtown was not through with her shopping and saw the car coming that she wished to ride home in, she would not hesitate to ask the driver to wait while she made another purchase or two, and the drivers never thought of refusing any request of this kind.'

Of Mr. Eddy, I asked, 'What did you mean a few minutes ago by saying that you asked your wife whether that car was waiting in front of your house because she wished to order something from downtown?'

'My wife, like all the other people living on or adjacent to the tracks, did a great deal of trading through the agency of the car drivers,' he answered. 'If my wife wanted a spool of thread or a sack of flour or almost anything else, she would listen for the tinkle of the bell that was suspended from the collar of the streetcar mule. When she heard that bell coming, she would go out and tell the driver what she wanted and give him the money to get it with. On the return trip, he would bring the stuff into the house and she would reward him with a small gratuity', concluded Mr. Eddy.

It is said that Mandy was retired after a number of years and was used by the company collector to ride home for lunch. Mandy was as reliable as a horse for personal transportation."

Mandy the Mule's Parade

The St. Louis journalist continued: "When the present up-to-date electric street car service was instituted three years ago, all El Paso united in a grand celebration. All the new cars were joined together and run about town all evening, and riding was free for as many people as could crowd aboard. There was a band and speech-making and a great pow-wow; but more impressive than anything else, in front of the electric car procession, was a flat car covered with wreaths and chain festoons of flowers, with Mandy riding. Mandy was far more the object of interest of that gladsome occasion than were the new cars." [1]

---

1. An old mystery may have finally been solved by the St. Louis article. In photographs of the occasion of the inaugural electric cars on January 11, 1902, a sign on the side of the flat car carrying Mandy read "In Appreciation for 35 Years of Dedicated Service." However, the El Paso mule cars ran only 20 years (1882–1902), so it appears that Mandy probably did see service in San Antonio or some other location before coming to El Paso.

Mandy the Mule's Parade 37

Figure 11: Mandy gets a ride on a flatcar pushed by a new electric car. The location is on Mills Street near the Sheldon Hotel. The date is January 11, 1902.

"The celebration ended at midnight, and the procession came to a halt in front of the new carbarns. Mandy was escorted from the car to the ground. Then Mandy gravely walked to a position alongside one of the new cars, turned so as to present her heels to the enemy, and proceeded to do her best to kick that modern improvement to smithereens. That was the first time Mandy was known to kick in all of her El Paso life, and the kindly endeavors of a score of men were necessary to get her away from the scene of demolition. The next day Mandy was sent out to an irrigated pasture, where she stood in grass and alfalfa knee high, there to end her days, with nothing to do but eat and drink. But eat she could not and drink she refused, and in a few days Mandy passed away—died, of grief because in the affections of her loved people of El Paso, she had been supplanted by an infernal invention which had no gratitude for kind words and caresses and no taste for apples and lumps of sugar. Dead, not from old age—because Mandy was not more than 50 or 60 years old—but dead from a broken heart.

There is a road leading out of El Paso to the southward. It is a good road and the much-traveled road is the favorite road with El Pasoans when they go pleasure driving. (Ed. note: probably County Road No.1 east toward the Lower Valley). One mile from town beside this road, there is a grave, and at the head of this grave there is a stone, not a board, but a sizable well-squared block of granite, and on the face of that stone is deeply carved one word, and that one word is Mandy. The grass grows green over that grave now, and flowers are often laid upon it—and many an El Paso woman when she alights from her carriage and bends over that grave and moistens the earth with a tear or two which springs from a loving memory.

Fine big cars whiz and whir through El Paso now, cars which would be a credit to the United Railways Company (of St. Louis), 22 of these every day, 30 on Sundays and more when special occasions warrant. Over in Juarez, the little city on the Mexican side of the line, they run and out to several suburban settlements as well. But many an old-timer, as he boards one those elegant electric cars, breathes a sigh for the good old days—and Mandy." (Ed. note: A romanticized and somewhat fanciful version, without doubt, but an interesting look at the popularity of the legend of Mandy.)

In an El Paso Electric Company publication[2] regarding the development of transportation in El Paso, there is a different of account of her last days which would seem to indicate that Mandy survived longer. She supposedly lived to make another public appearance, years later, by hauling the late Alves Dixon, General Superintendent of Railways, to Union Depot[3] when he left for a position at Baton Rouge, Louisiana in 1925. It was an occasion for a parade, and Mandy was supposedly the mule that pulled car No. 1 through the streets of El Paso with its dignitaries on board to Union Depot. The mule car was followed closely behind by a modern electric car with other guests. It was reported that she was balky and had to be led most of the way. This story may stretch credulity somewhat, since she supposedly had already been working for 35 years in 1902 at her retirement, which would make her at least 58 years old in 1925.

---

2. El Paso Electric Company, September, 1940.
3. Although known popularly as Union Depot, the official name was and is Union Passenger Station.

Figure 12: Parade in mule car for Alves Dixon, 1925, on San Francisco Street heading west toward Union Depot on electric car tracks.

Figure 13: Mule Car No. 1 at Union Depot in 1925 following parade honoring Alves Dixon. This is in the electric car era; however the mule car parade was a nostalgic event. Mule cars served the Southern Pacific and Santa Fe depots in their lifetime, but never Union Depot, which was built after the advent of electric cars.

A 1933 article reads as follows: "A.H. Reynolds[4] resurrected a clipping mounted on cardboard. It was from the *El Paso Herald* of September 10, 1901 and consisted of a joint partnership poem commemorating the passing of the mule car which had furnished transportation between El Paso and Juarez." (Ed. note: the intimation that there was one mule and one car is consistent throughout the history of the mule car system, but is, of course, mistaken). "Hewing the verses into form called for the perspiring efforts of Mr. Reynolds, his brother, the late Joshua S. Raynolds, and of Scott White, pioneer druggist and U.S. Marshal. Their united effort stood forth as follows:"

---

4. *El Paso Times,* March 30, 1933.

THE LAST MULE CAR

Let not Ambition mock his useful toil,
His lowly joys, or destiny befool,
Nor 'Modern Progress' hear with scornful simile,
The short and simple annals of the mule.

O'er a low born mule the setting sun,
Had thrown its latest ray,
When in his last strong agony,
He gave the a woeful bray-

"Zach, Zach, come back!" he cried in grief
"Do not, I beg, forsake me,
Or I'll be next a wienerwurst.
I've stood by you, now save me!

Come back, come back!" he cried in grief
Across the raging water,
"And I'll forgive your highland chief,
My daughter, o my daughter!"

Ah, what is friendship by a name?
A charm that lulls to sleep,
A shade that follows wealth or fame
And leave a mule to weep?

Alas, alas, he called too late.
The electric car moved in.
For what was mule or ancient car
To Zach, who'd got the tin?

When trusting mule flesh turns to folly
And learns too late that men betray,
What blind can hide that fiery trolley?
Whose hand shall wipe the tears away?

El Paeans all who had the call,
And you too, who had not,
Thank Goodrich-Davis all you wish,
But don't foretold Spot.

Ol' Spot who now by Zach forsaken
Departs the scene forever more-o,
He served his turn, some fun hath given
Vale! y Adios! El Mule Carro.

Written in 1901 at the end of the mule car era, the 1933 *Herald* editor adds this comment: "We suspect that in the above the casual reader will detect certain stanzas which the sweating geniuses seem to have cribbed out their collective memories of famous poems, but there was none to brand them with plagiarism."

Memories of Riding the Mule Car

Ed Pooley wrote a column titled *Side Bar Remarks* in the *El Paso Herald Post* in the fifties, and in one column[1] we find the following reader memories of riding the mule cars.

E.E. winter Sr., of 3601 Richmond Street, wrote: "As a boy back in 1889, I enjoyed many free rides on the little mule-drawn streetcar. We moved to Colorado but returned in 1896, and there were the same little cars and, no doubt, the same little mules with the same little bells jingling from their collars."

Mrs. Estella Duran-Vega, of 217 Polo Inn Road, tells of her grandmother, Mrs. Dolores Q. Veda de Duran, who came to El Paso from Chihuahua in the early 1880s. Says the granddaughter: "She says there was no Immigration Service then and people could cross over to Juarez and back, riding in the car pulled by the mule. My grandmother is around 91 and I guess you can say we are a pioneer family from way back. She was left a widow with five children in 1896."

Mrs. Zeola B. Day, of 2931 Frankfort Street, says: "I happened to be passing through El Paso on the way to Santa Fe over the weekend and stayed in the Plaza Hotel, and went to Juarez with a group of others staying at the hotel. This was in November 1901, when I was fifteen."

Mrs. Esther Darbyshire MacCallum, of 1815 Rio Grande Street, wrote: "I remember very well my mother taking me, my sister Marguerite, and my brothers Oliver and Spencer, in the little mule car when she went downtown to shop. Downtown for us was between the present sites of the Gateway Hotel and the Popular Dry Goods store. Often we children, with our little friends, were allowed, as a great treat, to ride around with Mr. Hill who would look after us. Whenever my mother and the other ladies on San Antonio Street needed a spool of thread, a steak for dinner, or some other thread or material for sewing, they would run out and meet Mr. Hill and ask him to do some shopping for them He was very accommodating."

---

1. *El Paso Herald Post*, September 28, 1955.

The Electric Car Era Approaches

Two gangs were employed to expedite the construction of the line, and salary expenditure for the preceding week was $2,200, not an insignificant amount for that time in El Paso. So near did the time seem for completion of the track that people were already expressing the fervent hope that, once the cars were running, they would not kill as many citizens as had those in Mexico City[1].

Things did not run smoothly, however, for the construction of the lines. There were labor difficulties and strikes among various building teams and arguments in city council over whether to use girder rail or the less expensive T-rail, but these were ironed out and construction continued. The company preferred the economy of the T-rail, but city council had asked for the safer girder rail which was less prone to derailments.

As the new electric street railway company was making definite strides in building the electric line, the old consolidated companies were still jockeying for position. Anson Mills and his associates petitioned for and were granted an extension of one year by Governor Ahumada to convert the streetcar lines in Juarez to electricity. It became increasingly evident that the El Paso Electric Railway would have to buy out the El Paso and Juarez Traction Company. Interestingly, by a 1900 report[2] of stockholders in the two companies, it was revealed that Mills and J.J. Gordon were the major stockholders in the two companies, respectively, the El Paso & Juarez Traction Company and the Santa Fe Street Railway Company. Zach White, by this time, only owned fifty shares in the Santa Fe Street Company.

In order to quell persistent rumors, the new company announced on July 27, 1901, that it had bought the El Paso and Juarez Traction Company, the Santa Fe Street Railway Company, the El Paso Gas, Electric Light, and Power Company, as well as 40% of the stock in the International Light and Power Company, for $500,000. All options were canceled. Zach White and J.J. Gordon, principal owners of the Santa Fe line, gas plant, and the old electric light plant, gave the

---

1. *El Paso Daily Herald,* December 27, 1901.
2. *Ibid,* November 14, 1900.

entire property to the new company, holding no stock at all. The sale had been negotiated by Felix Martinez who was to be one of the new directors. The new company had ended up paying $52,000 for the El Paso and Juarez Traction Company, down from the $200,000 asking price. The financier, J.J. Gordon, had been in El Paso for the sale, and upon its successful conclusion, left to return to Cincinnati. Upon his departure, however, he told local reporters that, although he was returning to the North, he would help build El Paso.

The Survival of No. 1

It should be noted here that the colloquial use in the present day is to refer to mule car No. 1 and the mule replica collectively as "Mandy". However, it should be reiterated that Mandy was the mule, not the car. She was the pet of the town, although there were many mules and thirteen or more cars. This segment will look at No. 1, the first car and the lone survivor of the mule car period from 1882 to 1902, when electric cars were introduced. As was mentioned earlier, the first mule car for El Paso (No. 1) was built by The John Stephenson Company of New York., probably in the late 1860's. At any rate, it came to El Paso in 1882 and figured prominently in the history of the city.

W. Floyd Payne, in his book, *Hunting in the High Mountains*[1], relates the following:

> "I feel proud that the Old Number One Mule Car was given to me in appreciation for the cooperation I extended in making several street franchises possible—this old car was moved into the back yard of my old home at 707 Myrtle Avenue and was used by my daughter Carolyn as a playhouse. When the old streetcar company sold out to the Stone & Webster Company in 1901–02, I helped in some way and the manager, Mr. Wadsworth, gave me Mule Car No. 1. He had it mounted on blocks in my back yard. It remained on that site for a number of years, and when my good friend, Mr. Alves Dixon, was General Superintendent of Railways, the old car was noticed by Mr. Ed J. Lawless. Upon the promotion of Mr. Dixon to Manager of the Baton Rouge Electric Company, Mr. Lawless and I made it possible for Mr. Dixon to ride to the railroad station in the old car. The day that Mr. Dixon left El Paso was marked by an event which I believe to be unique in streetcar history. After having been refurbished and a new truck frame installed[2], the old No. 1, which had been out of service for twenty-three years was again rolling and taking passengers. The car was first used in 1882. The car was placed on the track, and Mandy the Mule was once more hooked up to it as in days of yore

---

1. *Hunting in the High Mountains*, W. Floyd Payne, Gateway Press, El Paso, TX, 1940.
2. Author's note: In Mr. Payne's statement, there seems to be confirmation that the truck frame and running gear on the mule car as it is today is not the original. One can see where the rear springs are truncated.

(Ed. note: due to age, it seems doubtful that this really was the original Mandy). As sometimes happened, Mandy balked several times and it was necessary to lead her by the bridle for a good part of the journey. Both the mule and the car were dressed up for the occasion. Abe Carrasco, who had driven for 23 years, drove the car. Adolph Hoffman, an El Paso pioneer, was conductor, and on the car were many old-timers. A few years ago, I gave it back to them, and they repaired it so it looks like new. It is now in their yard on Magoffin Avenue[3]."

Mr. Payne continued:

"In recent conversations (1940) with Mr. Nelson of the Electric Company and Mr. J. Ed. Lawless, we planned to work out an arrangement with the city to place the old No. 1 car in one of the city parks or in a public place where the people of today may see for themselves this old relic of the past. The Electric Company will keep the old car in such a condition that it can be kept intact and in good shape for many years. The car is now in the barns of the Electric Company and Mr. Roy Nelson, president of the Electric Co., has promised me that nothing shall be left undone in keeping the old car preserved."

Following the somewhat circuitous trail of No. 1's wanderings over the years, it was apparently in good condition when returned to the Electric Company by W. Floyd Payne in the thirties. How then, did it end up in such a deplorable condition in the City Shops on Lee Street in 1953?

In a 1940 El Paso Electric Co. publication[4], there is an article entitled "From Mule Car to Motor Bus, History of Our Transportation Division". Contained therein is a statement regarding the mule car: "at the present time it is in our shops being repaired and restored to its original appearance. With the cooperation of Mr. Payne and Mr. J.B. Binkley, two our local citizens who are taking an interest in the matter with us, it is thought that some plan may be worked out to turn this old relic of bygone days over to the City to be preserved for its historic value."

J.B. Binkley was a part-time conductor for old No.1 in 1901. He told how he used to collect fares.

---

3. This appeared in Mr. Payne's book (previously foot-noted) which was published in 1940. We may assume "a few years ago" may have been the mid to late 1930's when he gave it back to the Electric Company.
4. El Paso Electric Co., Employee Information Leaflet, September, 1940.

> "I was 16 years old at the time", Mr. Binkley related. "I worked only on Sundays when the streetcars were crowded and they needed a conductor to help the driver. On the other days, the driver took the money. In 1901, I worked on the line that went from the Plaza up Mills Street, to Stanton Street and south on Stanton Street across the bridge to Comercio Street (now 16th of September) in Juarez. A lot of people piled on the car to go to Juarez on Sundays. I had strips of white and green paper. At that time, the Mexican peso was two for one dollar. When I collected five cents in American money, I punched the white slip. When I collected 10 cents in Mexican money, I punched the green slip...I had one pocket for U.S. money and one for Mexican money."

No. 1, and most of the mule cars, held 12–14 passengers and perhaps a few standees. Mr. Binkley recalled that the policemen in Juarez wore French-style uniforms and carried rifles. Constables often carried lanterns and tended to leave them in the middle of the tracks, causing Mr. Binkley to have to get down and remove them before the car could continue its journey.

The El Paso Electric Co. then reportedly donated the car to the City of El Paso. Roy Nelson, head of the Transportation Division of the Electric Company, stated in 1940[5] that, "through the efforts of J.B. Binkley, the car would be given to the City of El Paso" and that Mayor Anderson responded that the city would officially accept the car at the next Council meeting[6].

Historian Cleofas Calleros, writing for the *El Paso Times*[7], stated that J.B. Binkley had been the last owner of the car and had passed it on to the El Paso County Historical Society, who in turn would present it to the city. Although it is recognized that Mr. Binkley was the prime mover and instigator of the restoration, there is not found any documentary evidence of his physical possession of the car. There are two contradictory articles in the *El Paso Times* and *El Paso Herald-Post*[8], both in April 1940. In one, the car is recognized as belonging to Binkley who received it from the Electric Company and wanted to give it to the city if a suitable display area were provided. In the other article, dated the same day, it was noted that Mayor Anderson accepted the car directly from the Electric Company. It is probable that Mr. Binkley was the facilitator in this transaction.

---

5. *El Paso Times*, April 27, 1940.
6. The author's perusal of City Council minutes for May through September 1940, failed to locate any mention of mule car no.1, therefore, it is questionable that the transfer took place at that time.
7. *El Paso Times*, September 18, 1955
8. *El Paso Herald-Post*, April 27, 1940.

World War II came along, Mr. Binkley went to California to work in defense industries, and the City had other priorities to contend with. Materials were scarce and the car was moved to the back corral of the City shop on Lee Street, from its previous resting place in the streetcar barn lot on Cotton Street. El Paso City Lines had been the successor to the Electric Company in streetcar and bus operations. When Mr. Binkley returned from California after the war, he was dismayed to see it in a deteriorated condition. In 1953, he revived the efforts to restore the car and enlisted the efforts of the El Paso County Historical Society.

By 1953, No. 1 was being evicted from the Municipal Shops because of need for the space. The mule car had deteriorated considerably over the years and was in a dilapidated condition. When J.B. Binkley visited the city corral, he found No. 1 falling apart and tears came to his eyes. It was a cold, wintry day and an *El Paso Times* photographer took a picture of the hopeless heap of twisted iron and rotted boards. Jesse wrote a sad plea: his picture and that of the car was published.

Figure 14: Mule Car No. 1 in dilapidated condition in the early fifties in the City Corral on Lee St.

In the *El Paso Times*[9], it was reported that Alderman Hal Dean recommended the mule car be restored and placed in San Jacinto Plaza or City Hall Park. The city then approached Wesley Williams, City Lines Superintendent, who agreed

---

9. *El Paso Times*, May 5, 1953.

to accept the car for restoration. Herein is seen some further contradiction in newspaper accounts. Some indicate the restoration was done at the City Lines barn under Williams and others report it was done at the City Shops under L.L. Butterworth. It is possible it was a cooperative effort.

In any case, it was ready by September of 1955 and moved on a trailer by Southwestern Transfer to the Plaza for ceremonies. The casting of the mule was underwritten by Lodge 284 of the International Order of Odd Fellows and the plaster mold was made by Texas Western students James Goodman and Howard Hoffman. Unfortunately, they did not receive any recognition in the ceremonies or in the attendant publicity. The mule was cast in bronze from the mold which was said to have weighed about eight hundred pounds alone. The cast of Mandy was done at the Grubbs Foundry and was delayed as the original plaster cast had been ruined by a flood. The El Paso County Historical Society provided the funds for the shelter; the Popular Dry Goods provided the mannequin of "Pedro" the driver; the El Paso Brick Company donated the steel rails for the car track; Herman Blaugrand, the hat for the Mexican driver; Mrs. R.C. Thomas donated the swingle tree for mule harness.

There apparently was some lapse of responsibility from the City Parks Department as a letter[10] from Chris P. Fox of the State National Bank shows he sent five checks payable to different members of the Parks Department for their work on the shelter. Mr. Fox also expressed his disappointment that the commitment by former City Alderman Ernie Ponce, that the city would build the shelter, was not kept.

The ceremony was held downtown in the Plaza on September 14, 1955 to place No. 1 on display in the park, surrounded by an iron fence. According to the *El Paso Times*[11],

---

10. Letter, Chris P. Fox to Mr. Bryce Lambert, dated June 24, 1957.
11. *El Paso Times*, September 15, 1955.

Figure 15: newspaper article on the placement of No. 1 in San Jacinto Plaza in September of 1955.

"A parade preceded the presentation ceremony. It began at the City shops at Lee and Magoffin, where the streetcar was restored, and proceeded down San Antonio to North Oregon, and up Oregon to the Plaza at Main Street. The Sheriff's Posse escorted the streetcar and mule, mounted on a truck. After casting in iron, the mule weighed 2,100 lbs. Descendants of pioneers with interest in the original streetcar companies rode in the restored car. Among these were Brig. Gen. and Mrs. W.J. Glasgow of Magoffin Avenue. Mrs. Glasgow is a daughter of Joseph Magoffin who was mayor when the first streetcar franchise was granted. Also in the old car was Mrs. Charlotte Massey, grand-daughter of Zach T. White, pioneer mule car operator."

The car was presented to the city by the President of the El Paso Historical Society, Paul A Heisig, Jr., and accepted by the Mayor, Tom Rogers. Chris Fox was the Master of Ceremonies. Sometime after the ceremony, "passengers" cut from cardboard and painted with faces, were inserted in the windows of the car.

By 1968, the city had plans for the renovation of San Jacinto Plaza which did not include Mandy and No. 1. This news was particularly upsetting to Mr. Binkley, who was fearful that the car would be stored out of view and allowed to deteriorate as had previously happened during WWII.

In 1969, the whole display was moved over to Cleveland Square with a new facility, which was dedicated on October 21, 1969. The car had a cover and an iron fence around it, but it was open on the sides to the elements. By 1985, it was in need of restoration once again and the job was accepted by David Carrasco,

Director of the Job Corps Center[12]. Over several months, the students at the center did a cosmetic restoration under supervision. However, trolley buffs inspecting No.1, state that the car would not be operational since the body is not firmly attached to the truck (wheel and bolster arrangement), the brake rigging is missing, and the lack of flanging on the wheels would not allow the car to stay on the track. The leather harness and riggings have long since disappeared, although these were present in a photo taken in the late seventies.

In 2003, it appears that Mandy and No. 1 will need to find a new home, as the Cleveland Square display site will be in the way of library expansion and the new History Museum building. It is expected that Mandy will be displayed somewhere in the Union Plaza area, although the author contends that a more historically appropriate placement would be at the Magoffin Home, on its original route, or in a transportation-related museum.

---

12. *El Paso Herald-Post,* January 16, 1985.

PART II
The El Paso Suburban Railway To Tobin Place

Land Developers and Their New Towns

With the invention and development of the electric streetcar by Frank J. Sprague in 1888, public transit systems grew exponentially as electric street railways began to replace the plodding mule and horse cars of the late 1800s. In the early 1900s, electric street railways flourished across the United States. An outgrowth of this new method of urban transit was the electric interurban railway, connecting urban centers of shorter distances with schedules which were often more convenient and frequent than those provided by the steam railroads. While some interurbans were simply extensions of city street railways and used the same equipment and track construction techniques, others were built to steam railroad standards and used heavier, high-speed electric cars which could, and often did, travel along sides of country roads at speeds of sixty miles per hour or higher.

While the majority of interurbans were located in the East and the Midwest near large population centers, they were also built in the South and the West, and Texas was no exception. There were electric interurbans connecting Houston and Galveston, Dallas to Fort Worth, Waco, Corsicana, Denton, Denison, and Terrel. In the far west of Texas, El Paso had two suburban railways, one steam powered and one electric powered, the latter being a true interurban.

In 1902, El Paso was a bustling railroad and mining industry center of approximately 20,000 population, (the 1900 Federal Census had reported 15,906). In that same year, El Paso had taken a major step forward in converting from a mule car to an electric street railway system. Over the next decade, the streetcars would play a major role in the development of the neighborhoods of the city. By 1912, cars ran to all parts of the city including Washington Park, Union Depot, the Smelter, Sunset Heights, Fort Bliss, Government Hill, Kern Place, Arizona Street, Highland Park, Manhattan Heights, Second Ward, and Ciudad Juarez. About this time, there began to develop interest in having the car lines extend further out to the more outlying areas including parts of the Lower Valley and Ysleta. Ysleta, the focal point of cotton farms and orchards in the valley, had actually been the first county seat and had both historical and agricultural significance.

Earlier, however, in 1907, there arose a rather interesting real estate development called Tobin Place, named for its developer, Frank R. Tobin, in what would later be known as the Northeast section of El Paso. Tobin and his associate, Frank B. Hadlock, hired Louis M. Carl[1], a noted civil engineer and designer to develop the property. "Mr. Carl had many years experience in the laying out of town sites, and his work on the Tobin properties was considered one of the finest pieces of civic engineering in the Southwest."

Tobin advertised his development as "El Paso's Queen Suburb, located beyond Fort Bliss, on the El Paso and Southwestern Railroad, on the Mesa, where El Paso should have been located." Tobin and Hadlock were associates in this ultimately unsuccessful undertaking and later would work together on the interurban to Ysleta. Hadlock, in an interview with the *El Paso Times*[2] at age 74 in 1956, recalled that the concept was well founded because floods periodically did great damage to Central El Paso prior to the construction of Elephant Butte Dam, which was completed in 1916. Hadlock remembered flood waters in the lobby of the old Sheldon Hotel, which was destroyed by fire in 1929.

---

1. Interview by Genevieve Overman of Mrs. Frank Tobin On Jan. 28, 1936.
2. *El Paso Times*, Feb. 5, 1956.

The Development of Tobin Place

Tobin and his business partners bought a section and a half of land from the El Paso and Northeastern Railway[1] located northeast of El Paso in the desert across the tracks and farther out from Fort Bliss. At that time, there was no development in the northeast desert other than a few isolated ranches. Tobin's engineer, Mr. Carl, subdivided the property into residential lots, which sold for ten dollars apiece. Business lots went for fifty dollars each. Even that small amount could be paid in payments. Tobin had somewhat grandiose plans for businesses, stores, machine shops, a water system, and all the appurtenances of a developed community. His ads claimed that water was available at the same price as in El Paso, i.e., 20 cents for 1,000 gallons. He correctly predicted that the El Paso Country Club would build a golf course nearby.

Initially, at the opening of the development in 1907, Tobin and Hadlock rented special trains from the El Paso & Southwestern at $250 each to carry prospective buyers from the new Union Depot downtown out to Tobin Place, where a siding was provided by the railroad. Later, a White steam automobile[2] was used to transport buyers from the end of the Fort Bliss streetcar line to the development. When this arrangement proved to be unsatisfactory and not particularly efficient, he began to shop around for another type of transportation for visitors. Tobin then returned to his hometown of St. Louis where he purchased what was known as a steam dummy. It was essentially a steam locomotive fitted with a trolley-like body, able to carry passengers by itself or to pull one or two passenger cars. There were at least two open-vestibule coaches built for the El Paso Suburban Railway (Tobin's name for his railroad). These two coaches included an express door in the middle, apparently to handle packages or express.

---

1. El Paso & Northeastern later became part of the El Paso & Southwestern RR.
2. Ed. Note: The White Steam Automobile was similar to the more notable Stanley Steamer.

Figure 16: Frank R. Tobin's steam dummy on the El Paso Suburban Railway line to Tobin Place.

The El Paso Suburban Railway

Tobin's idea was to construct his own rail line from the end of the Fort Bliss streetcar line out to Tobin Place, a distance of about five miles. In order to build his own rail line to Tobin Place along the east side of the El Paso & Southwestern Railroad right of way, Tobin had to obtain permission from Washington to build on Ft. Bliss property. Consent was obtained and the rail was laid at a cost of $40,000 for grading, and for tie and rail construction. Rail was light in contrast to the next door steam railroad, the El Paso & Southwestern. Likewise, the equipment was smaller, slower, and cheaper to operate than that of a regular railroad. The only similarity is that both were standard gauge, that being four feet, eight and one-half inches between the rails.

Fares were a nickel, which included a transfer to or from the El Paso Street Railway to any part of town. There were two open vestibule cars of the late 1880s style, which were pulled behind the steam dummy when traffic warranted. Mr. R.D. Paschal, in a letter to the *Ask Ann Carroll*[1] column in the local newspaper, related that when he was 10 or 11 years old, his father was the manager of the Nations Ranch near Tobin Place. He would stay in town with his mother during the week to go to school, but on Friday afternoons he would go out to the ranch to help his father. He and a friend, whose father also worked on the ranch, would catch the 3:30 p.m. Ft. Bliss streetcar to get to the end of the line in time to catch the 4 p.m. *Tobin Limited*. If he missed that particular Ft. Bliss streetcar, he and his friend would have to walk the remaining five miles from Fort Bliss to the Tobin and Nations properties.

In an undated letter to the editor of the *El Paso Herald Post*, Mr. D.A. Downs of Alamogordo recalled, "you took the Ft. Bliss streetcar to the turn-around at the end of the line. There stood the *Tobin Limited*, panting and ready to go. The track ran out to Tobin which was about five miles north on the east side of the El Paso & Southwestern main line to Alamogordo. The turn-around out there was at its terminus roughly across the S.P. tracks from the El Paso Natural Gas company pumping station. The Tobin special ran three trips in the morning and

---

1. *El Paso Herald Post*, Dec. 20, 1972.

three in the afternoon. On slow days, I worked my way by firing the locomotive. Joe Burris taught me how; I also blew the whistle in a scream as we passed the *Golden State Limited* doing about sixty miles an hour while we were fooling along at about 15 miles per hour. Joe Burris lived in Ysleta and died there."

Figure 17: open vestibule cars of the El Paso Suburban Railway on the Tobin Place line.

A few houses were built, but probably no more that four or five in addition to the Tobin home. Tobin's widow sadly related the tale that, after her husband's death, their fine home was vandalized by unknowns and later further ruined by its use by the military on maneuvers. Unfortunately, sales never matched the developer's costs and after Tobin's death from an upper respiratory infection in 1914, following a trip to St. Louis, Tobin Place failed. The town site apparently was not further developed, so it was not surprising that many credit buyers defaulted on their payments, allowing the land to revert back to mesquite and desert. Perhaps it was simply too far from the centers of commerce clustered around the confluence of the railroads and highways at the Pass of the North.

In 1954, Tobin's widow, who never remarried, and who was the El Paso County Treasurer for many years, sold the land to the real estate firm of Haynesworth and Huckleberry, who developed the neighborhoods of Nations-Tobin. In the present-day Northeast section of El Paso, there is a Nations-Tobin Park and a street named after Marie Tobin. In addition, Frank Tobin was responsible for a considerable amount of development including West Ysleta and Tobin's Fourth Addition, where he was living at the time of his death. It was said that Frank R. Tobin was the first private individual to build a skyscraper, that being a nine-story building in St. Louis.

Frank Tobin's El Paso Suburban Railway was not a true interurban in the sense of being powered by electricity; however it did fulfill the requirements of light rail and urban to suburban transport. Interestingly, the wheel arrangement on the Tobin railway's steam dummy was an unusual type not known to be used elsewhere. Recently, divers working in a bay in the New York and New Jersey area discovered two very similar locomotives at the bottom of the bay. No one knows where they came from or how they came to be there.

From John G. Oechnser[2] is this story: "I bought one of the lots at the Tobin town site for ten dollars in 1908. Frank Pittman, County Clerk, witnessed the notarizing of the deed. I held that lot for 34 years and in 1942 during Word War Two the United States Government took it over and paid me 73 cents for it. During the 34 years I owned it, I paid taxes on the lot, so you see, it was not exactly a profitable deal."

---

2. *Ask Ann Carroll, El Paso Herald Post*, Dec. 8, 1972.

PART III

The Interurban to Ysleta (The Rio Grande Valley Traction Company)

Developing an Interurban to Ysleta

From about the time Tobin Place began in 1907, there was agitation among the public and civic leaders in El Paso and the Lower Valley to construct an interurban from downtown east to Ysleta and perhaps beyond. Frank Hadlock and Frank Tobin both were also involved in this project initially, although Hadlock was to withdraw later on in disagreement with the Stone and Webster Corporation of Boston, who would ultimately complete the project. A number of El Paso pioneers and influential businessmen were pushing for the interurban including Richard F. Burges, James McNary, Hadlock, and Felix Martinez.

As often was the case, the proposed interurban line would enter and leave the city over existing street railway trackage, which would require the cooperation of the El Paso Street Railway, a Stone and Webster property. In this case, the western terminus would be the Union Depot and the line would travel via Overland Street to San Antonio Street, thence out the Washington Park line via Myrtle and Alameda Streets to the end of the El Paso Street Railway line at Alameda and Conception Streets. This was common practice in interurban routing. As an example, the large Texas Electric Railway accessed its Dallas terminal over the tracks of the Dallas Street Railways.

Several investment companies were interested, including one from Seattle and one from London, England; however, the parent company of the El Paso Street Railway, the Stone and Webster Corporation of Boston, was in the best position to construct the line. Two plans were proposed to the public. In one scheme, an independent company would lay the track and build a power plant, necessitating a large outlay of capital funds. In the other plan, the work would be done in conjunction with Stone and Webster as they already had carbarns, equipment, and construction expertise in place. Sensing that success in securing the line was near, local engineers surveyed the line, and most of the land for the right of way was secured prior to construction. Stone and Webster then announced they would build the line if the citizens of El Paso would raise $60,000 toward the cost of the line.

During the month of February, 1912, H.S. "Harry" Potter, Winchester Cooley, and Mayor C.E. Kelley, went to Washington to lobby for a larger Fort Bliss, thence on to Boston to meet with the Stone and Webster people. At the end of that meeting, it was noted by Cooley[1] that "an interurban railway would not be a paying proposition for at least the first year, and the outlay would be heavy. For this reason, the Stone and Webster people would not be willing to take up the building of the interurban at this time without a bonus[2] of $60,000." The line would run from the end of the Washington Park line to Ysleta. Extensions beyond Ysleta to Clint, Fabens, and Tornillo, had been considered at one time, but were determined to be not feasible initially. In a classic text, *Electric Interurban Railways in America* [3], Hilton and Due stated that an extension to Fabens was cut back to Ysleta in 1918 and the line to Ysleta was abandoned in 1932. In reality, although there was discussion of a line to Fabens, it was never built. Additionally, the line to Ysleta was cut back to Ascarate in 1925, not 1932.

In a March 1912, meeting at the Chamber of Commerce, a letter from Stone & Webster was read which reiterated the $60,000 bonus requirement and pointed out that a fifty foot right-of-way along the route would have to be secured. In the letter, Stone and Webster agreed to provide a frequency of a least one car per hour during the day, with a greater frequency if traffic warranted. The line would be incorporated as the Rio Grande Valley Traction Company, a wholly owned Stone & Webster subsidiary. Everyone present seemed willing to help accomplish these goals. There was a committee selected to help in the raising of the bonus and in obtaining the rights of way needed. J.A. Smith was the chairman and members were J.G. McNary, Frank R. Tobin, R.L. Dorbandt and Felix Martinez. Although Tobin's own northeast development had failed, he played a major role in the development of the Ysleta interurban line.

By May of 1912, only $8,600 of the bonus money had been raised. Mr. Tobin reported that the right of way already obtained was valued at $18,000. In a scheme to raise more funds, 50,000 souvenir tickets for the interurban were printed to be sold to the public for one dollar each. The tickets indicated they were good for one round trip from either terminus and advertised "including admission to the Southwestern Ostrich Farm. Visit the old historic town of Ysleta, first county seat of El Paso County. See the old Mission and boost the interurban. Good at any time within one year of the sale date." The ticket also

---

1. *The El Paso-Ysleta Interurban*, George E. W. Love, 1953.
2. Ed. note: The "bonus" was to be raised locally.
3. *Electric Interurban Railways in America,* George W. Hilton & John F. Due, Stanford University Press, Stanford, CA 1960.

included the caveat "Failure to have said interurban in operation within two years from June 1, 1912, entitles the holder to surrender this ticket to T. M. Wingo, Trustee, or his successor, and procure one dollar therefore."

Civic and fraternal organizations including the Shriners, the Elks, the Beavers, the Knights of Columbus, the Moose, and the Toltec Club all joined in to sell the tickets to the public, but fell considerably short of the goal. Stone and Webster announced on June 3rd that the bonus requirement had been reduced to $15,000, of which $12,000 had already been raised. By June 5th, the news arrived that a contract with Stone and Webster to build the line for the bonus and the right of way had been completed. However, it was necessary for Mssrs. Frank Tobin, Robert Dorbandt, W. Cooley, Lamar Davis, J. Wyatt, Walter Clayton, Felix Martinez, T.M. Wingo, James McNary, and J.A. Smith to sign a pledge to make good the remaining $3,000, personally, if necessary.

The petition for a franchise was submitted to the County Commissioner's Court on June 10, 1912. The commissioners, however, felt that the franchise as presented was too sweeping and vague. They preferred to approve an exact route and wanted to be able to specify a timeline for the completion of the construction. The court worded the franchise to say that "This franchise is granted upon the condition that the grantees shall commence construction of said line of railway from the eastern limits of the city of El Paso to a point within a half of a mile of the old church at Ysleta, Texas, within six months and shall complete the same within 18 months." The County Commissioners visited Ysleta on June 11th to inspect the town in connection with the interurban, and were assured by the local residents that the line could enter the town on any street it wanted. They were even willing to have the line enter the village on the main road to the old church. The commissioners thereby granted the franchise with authority to extend beyond Ysleta in the county if needed.

Deeds were finally secured by December, 1912. The Engineering department of Stone & Webster cooperated by furnishing unsigned deeds drawn up to show a legal description of the right of way, and committee members then went out to secure the signatures of the property owners. Mark Lowd was selected as Chief Engineer and the total cost of the line including rolling stock and all accessories, was to be $236,000 estimated. There were subcontracts let and the firm of Dudley and Orr put fifty teams of mules and horses with laborers to work grading. They were under contract to finish the grading in forty days.

Construction Begins

The El Paso Morning Times of February 4, 1913, reported on the ceremony of the turning of the first shovel of dirt, the honor being given to Frank R. Tobin. The ceremonies took place just below the Clardy tract, about one half mile east of Washington Park, approximately at the present location of Alameda and Concepcion Streets.

The traction company leased a block of property in the Cotton Addition near the existing carbarn to store construction materials. The Texas & Pacific Railway cooperated and connected a spur to the company's tracks so that carloads of material could be routed directly to the end of track without having to be transloaded. Materials used in the construction as recorded in company records, and as researched by George E.W. Love, included 23,237 pine ties, 915 tons of 60 lb. rail, and 21,863 lbs. of trolley wire, to mention a few. One bridge was constructed along the line, that being over the Franklin Canal approximately one block from the Val Verde stop (Alameda and Concepcion).

Figure 18: Interurban right of way along the side of County Road No.1.

As can be seen in the preceding photo, the grading and fill of the roadbed was minimal in the interest of economy and time.

The interurban did not follow the Franklin Canal all the way to Ysleta as is frequently reported. A legal description of the right of way is found in the El Paso County Archives[1] dating to when the Rio Grande Valley Traction Company was dissolved in 1929, and the property sold to other utilities. The route through present Ascarate was along the side of County Road No. 1, which became U.S. Highway 80 and is now Alameda Street. It was at this point that some controversy arose between the company and Frank Hadlock, one of the early proponents of the line. The company wanted to double track the line in front of Mr. Hadlock's property, about where Jefferson High School is today, but Hadlock objected, stating that the company had not obtained the rights to his property and refused them access. The engineer, a Mr. James White, seems to have solved the problem by simply laying the disputed trackage at night without Hadlock's knowledge. No other difficulties were encountered and track was being laid at the rate of one-half mile per day. Track along Alameda on the Park line was initially on the south side of the street, but was later double-tracked in the center median. This was the route the interurban would use to approach the city from the East. There was ample precedence for this type of arrangement.

---

1. El Paso County Archives, Book 525, page 91.

Power and Equipment

Most streetcar lines and many interurbans were operated at 600 volts DC. To pass direct current voltage over long distances involved significant losses of power, therefore most systems used substations along the longer lines, where higher voltages could be "stepped down" to 600 volts DC. A case in point was El Paso Street Railway's (later El Paso Electric's) substation on the Fort Bliss line on Copia near Altura. The same was true of the interurban, there being two substations, one at Valverde already in use on the Park line, and a new one built at the West Ysleta stop, still in use today by the electric company.

Figure 19: One of the four St. Louis interurban cars ordered for the Rio Grande Valley Traction in a builder's photo from the St. Louis Car Company, 1913.

In the builder's photo above of No. 4, by the St. Louis Car Company, it is noted that these were typically taken at the factory with a white canvas to block out the background, and without trolley poles which were usually mounted after the car arrived on the purchaser's property. The Rio Grande Valley Traction Company ordered four interurban passenger cars from the St. Louis Car Company. These were high speed 44-passenger cars and were numbered 1 to 4. The cars were single enders which meant they had to be turned at each end of the line on a wye track or a loop. A loop was available at the Union Depot end and it is believed a wye track was used at Ysleta. High speeds were obtainable with the 200 hp motors. The cars were generally able to make the Union Depot to Ysleta run in 45 minutes. There would be a 15-minute layover and the car would make the return run. On weekends and holidays, there was often a trailer car carried, which was not powered, but supplied additional passenger capacity. An express or freight motor was obtained and given the No. 50. It was seldom used, however, and was soon sent to another Stone & Webster property, the Galveston-Houston interurban.

Figure 20: Interurban motor pulling a trailer at speed between El Paso and Ysleta.

Service was to begin after passing of an ordinance by the City of El Paso to allow the operation of the cars on city streets. The ordinance passed City Council easily and the traction company was given the right to operate on Alameda, Myrtle, San Antonio, Texas, Campbell, Mills, El Paso, and Cotton Streets as well as the use of the Cotton Street carbarns. The inaugural runs of the service were August 27, 1913. Two of the new cars in dark green and gold leaf lettering pulled up in front of the Electric Building at five in the afternoon and a party of prominent businessmen were treated to the first ride down the valley. The cars ran through to Ysleta, and then returned to the Knoblach Ranch where a special barbecue had been prepared. Regular passenger service started soon thereafter.

There were eight platforms and shelters built for stops. The regular stops were Val Verde, Bosque, Awbrey, Franklin, Porcher, Cadwallder, Cinecue Park, Valdespino, West Ysleta, and Ysleta. Fares ranged from 10 cents to Val Verde up to 30 cents for the ride all the way to Ysleta. Cars left on the hour from each end of the line between 6 a.m. and 11 p.m. and passed each other at the midway point. There were four crews of two men each, one a motorman who operated the car and the conductor who collected fares and was in charge. Residents along the way so appreciated the service, that mothers would often flag down a passing car to hand the trainmen pieces of cake or pie.

El Pasoans who rode the interurban recalled that the seats were high-backed leather and very comfortable. There was a smoking compartment at the front of the car where men congregated to smoke and talk politics. It was said no self-respecting lady would dare ride in the smoking compartment. Crews were courteous and patient and often waited as a would-be passenger sprinted towards the car. Before the construction of a high school in the Lower Valley, some students rode the interurban into town to go to the original El Paso High on Arizona and Campbell Streets. They had the option of getting off at about Myrtle and Cotton, then walking north for a couple of miles or getting off in downtown and transferring to the Arizona Street carline.

West Ysleta was advertised as a lovely development offering the best of rural living with the conveniences of the city. Much like Tobin Place, it failed to attract a great many buyers and remained mostly rural in nature. The completion of the Elephant Butte Dam and the Elephant Butte Irrigation District led to high hopes that development would take place in the Lower Valley at a faster pace.

The Decline of the Interurban

The problem was that the interurban served primarily a rural area and the town of Ysleta had not kept up with El Paso's growth. Unfortunately, although the service was a boon to the residents of the valley, there were too few riders overall, and as early as 1921, the traction company ordered five single truck Birney streetcars from the St. Louis Car Company to replace the big interurbans. The advantage to the company in using the 21-passenger Birneys was primarily one of economy of operation, in addition to the fact that it was a one-man car. The motorman collected the fares as the passengers boarded. The disadvantage, in the eyes of the patrons, was that the single truckers rode quite roughly and had the tendency buck and dip over uneven track, earning the nickname "Toonerville Trolley". Even that economy measure could not save the interurban and it was cut back to Ascarate in 1925.

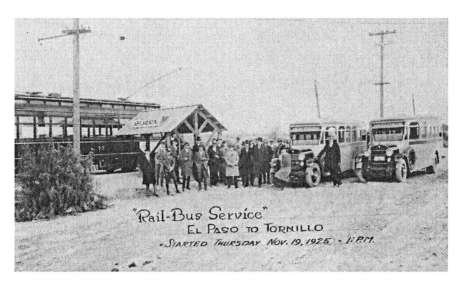

Figure 21: The King Cotton Express at the Ascarate interurban shelter.

The *King Cotton Express* bus then met the interurban at Ascarate and continued as far as Tornillo. With passenger service declining by the early 1920s, two of the interurbans were sent to the Galveston-Houston property where they served until 1936 on Houston's Park Place line. With the advent of the single truck Birneys, the remaining two interurbans served variously on the Fort Bliss and Juarez lines, often pulling unpowered trailers for more passenger capacity. Residents of the Lower Valley were sad to see the big, fast, comfortable interurbans go, but understood the profit-loss realities of the parent company.

At its maximum, the Rio Grande Valley Traction Company operated 9.34 miles in the county and 3.49 miles in the city. Along the county road leaving El Paso was 0.775 miles of right of way. On private right-of-way was another 8.113 miles and on the Main Street of Ysleta was 0.454 miles. There were 0.5 miles of side tracks and wyes.

In 1929, the Ascarate track was cut back to Concepcion Street, and the Park line streetcar terminated at the Del Camino Courts. Of the two remaining interurban cars, they were found in the 1960's serving as tenement apartments in a block on Alameda Street, where it once ran. Thus ended a colorful chapter in El Paso transit history.

Figure 22: Two derelict interurban cars after serving as apartments on a lot on Alameda Street in the 1960's near the present day R.E. Thomason Hospital.

Conclusion

With the coming of the second transcontinental railroad in 1881, the path to the sister cities of Paso del Norte, Mexico, and El Paso, Texas, became wide open to the rest of the world. In the horse-and-buggy era of the 1880s, the mule cars supplied the first mass public transit this part of the nation had ever seen. From that first few hundred that crossed the bridge on a mule-drawn streetcar on the first day in 1882, to the two million that rode the electric streetcar across the river in its last year of cross-border operation in 1973, these conveyances touched the lives of almost every citizen.

In just twenty years, El Paso was transformed from a wayside traveler's rest with adobe buildings and dusty streets to a metropolitan city with a good start on paved roads, a water system, indoor plumbing, electricity, and modern electric streetcars. With five railroads connecting El Paso to every part of the country and Mexico, and an electric street railway reaching out to new neighborhoods, the growth of the city was extraordinary. El Paso became an agricultural, commercial, and mining industry center of the region, at the same time that Fort Bliss established a strong military presence in the area. As in earlier centuries, with the missionaries, the Spaniards, and the Indians, the *Pass of the North* became a gateway in and out of Mexico. The Southern Transcontinental route offered the best weather conditions for travelers on rail or on highway. It is not at all surprising that the city experienced phenomenal growth during that time.

Historians and writers, in the past, have found it too easy to credit the automobile with the fluidity and mobility of early Twentieth Century society, but a significant amount of credit for the growth of the suburbs and neighborhoods of El Paso should go to the development of streetcar routes from 1902 to 1925. In those days, roads off the main highways were often rutted, dusty, and almost impassable in rainy weather. The electric streetcar overcame those obstacles and carried El Pasoans to all parts of the city in all directions. There were routes to: Juarez, Second Ward, Hipodromo, Sunset Heights, Kern Place, the Smelter, Union Depot, Arizona Street, Highland Park, Manhattan Heights, William Beaumont Army Hospital, Fort Bliss, Government Hill, Richmond Terrace, El Paso High School, Washington Park, and Ysleta. The streetcars played an immensely important role in the development of the neighborhoods of El Paso and made it possible for families to shop, to go to work, and to find entertainment.

About the Author

Ron Dawson has served in various railroad and historical capacities including: officer or board member of the Southwest Chapter of the Railway & Locomotive Historical Society, the Paso Del Norte Streetcar Preservation Society, the City of El Paso's Railroad and Industrial Archeology Board, and the Railroad and Transportation Museum of El Paso. He has authored several articles on streetcars and has produced the El Paso Streetcar Calendar over a number of years. He currently is developer and webmaster for websites for El Paso Streetcars, Railroading in the El Paso Southwest, the Pioneer Air Lines History Page, and the website for the Railroad and Transportation Museum of El Paso.

You are invited to visit the websites of these organizations:

Railroad and Transportation Museum of El Paso: elpasorails.org
Southwest Chapter, R&LHS: trainweb.org/ep-sw/index1.htm
El Paso Streetcars Home Page: trainweb.org/elpasocars/index.htm

Friends of the Railroad and Transportation Museum of El Paso

Interest and support is solicited for the *Friends of the Railroad and Transportation Museum of El Paso* in this important development phase. It is anticipated that the museum will have an interpretive exhibit space adjacent to the El Paso & Southwestern locomotive No. 1 in the new Union Plaza Terminal Building. It is possible Mule Car No. 1 may be exhibited at the same venue, although no decision has been finalized at this time. Volunteer docents from the friends will need to staff that facility. In addition, the museum will continue its efforts to obtain a historical railroad station with trackage for museum exhibits and operations. For membership information, please contact the curator, Prince McKenzie at 915-422-3420.

Acknowledgements

Mr. R.L. Thomas, for his research and archival work on El Paso streetcars.

Mr. Patrick Rand of Cloudcroft, who provided copies of early mule car company charters and minutes of board meetings which were greatly appreciated.

Mr. George E.W. Love, whose research conducted in 1953 when many of the individuals were still living, and many of the records still accessible, was an invaluable aid in this project.

Mr. Henry Leinbach, whose seminal work on the transit history of El Paso opened the door and provided the basis for further research to begin the process.

With appreciation to these organizations who made their archives available:

The Railroad and Transportation Museum of El Paso
The Southwest Chapter of the Railway and Locomotive Historical Society
The Paso del Norte Streetcar Preservation Society
El Paso Public Library, Border Heritage Section
University of Texas at El Paso, Special Collections
El Paso County Historical Society

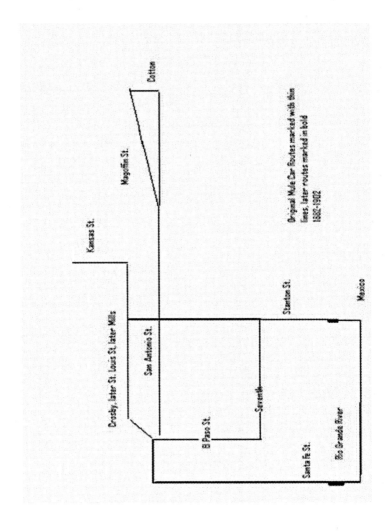

Photograph Credits

Otis Aultman photographs from:
    Collection of Ronald E. Dawson
    Collection of the Paso del Norte Streetcar Preservation Society
    Collection of the late Millard G. McKinney
    Border Heritage Center, El Paso Public Library

Unknown photographer photos from:
    Collection of the Paso del Norte Streetcar Preservation Society

0-595-29623-8

Printed in the United States
34795LVS00005B/514-564